The Sea

Hilaire Wood

Brigit's Forge

Published by Brigit's Forge
Gelli Fach, Clos y Ceiliog,
Llandre, SY24 5AN

Artwork by Jenny Fell ©

ISBN: 978-0-9574106-0-2

Cover and page design by Hilaire Wood. Typesetting by Elaine Sharples,
typesetter.org.uk. Printed by Cambrian Printers Ltd., Llanbadarn Road,
Aberystwyth, Wales, SY23 3TN Tel: 01970 627111

Acknowledgements

Thanks are due to the editors of the following publications where some of these poems first appeared: the Machynlleth based journal *Valleys*, the anthology *Out of the Ash* produced by the Aberystwyth Writing Project and *A River of Stones* from Writing Our Way Back Home. Special thanks are also due to the Welsh Women's Press, Honno, for choosing 'Rapunzel' as poem of the month for their website.

I should also like to thank Jenny Fell for her beautiful artwork; Karoline Deck for her encouragement in times past; also all my good friends and the Monday arts centre group, especially Janet Thomas, for their support; the Word Distillery poets for their invaluable advice and Jane Edmonds, Dylan Jones, Jane MacNamee and Michael Nobbs for assistance with the production of this pamphlet.

About the Author

Hilaire Wood was born and brought up on the east coast of Yorkshire. She studied English at Southampton University and then lived for several years in Deià, Mallorca, and in London, where she worked for Camden Libraries. In 1977 she moved to Wales to attend the College of Librarianship in Aberystwyth. After some years working in the university library she retrained as a homeopath and ran a successful practice for 20 years.

Having retired, she returned to poetry, her first love, and has been working with the Word Distillery poetry group based in Aberystwyth Arts Centre. Her poems have appeared in a number of anthologies and she also publishes work on Celtic mythology and religion. She lives near the sea in West Wales and has a son, a daughter-in-law and two grandchildren.

For more information, go to:
storingmagic.blogspot.com
musingsfromgellifach.blogspot.com
word-distillery.blogspot.com

Contents

To Dylan and Leila

and to all who read this book:

The merciful word, the singing word and the good word,
may the power of these three sacred things
be on you now and for evermore.

To Brigit

Irish goddess of poetry, healing and smithcraft

You walked out of ancient mists
bringing light to my path,
blessing with fire
restoring the life with the flame.

Clothed in your grace,
I follow your footsteps
to the place where mysteries merge
and the shapes behind myth
are revealed as truth.

Your presence soothes
and sharpens memory;
you are my maker of song,
the radiant flame of gold
that illuminates the land
beyond the ninth wave,
that forges a sword of light
to penetrate, to heal.

Kneeling at your well
I drink of your mystery;
the waters of the sun
flood my skull
with sacred fire,
flowing with light,
my spirit sings of the deep.

The Journey

Traveller, there is no path; the path is made by walking.
By walking you make the path and when you look back
you'll see the road you'll never walk again.

Antonio Machado

It's disconcerting how the mist falls so quickly,
becomes a clinging wraith that insinuates itself
between you and the path.

You stay on intimate terms with your own feet,
the only objects visible in front of your eyes,
a testament that you are not blind.

The mist seethes and murmurs,
gestures and shape-shifts,
opens up a chunk of moorland –
rushes, a sheep's skull, a flash of quartz –
invites, cajoles, entices, threatens
footfalls to oblivion.

You are locked into yourself,
the perimeters of your body the only surety,
standing, as if perished,
a grey shape on the hillside.

Traveller, there is no path, you make the path by walking.

Honeycomb

Around me the intense buzzing of the bee,
busy on the yellow rue blossoms,
gathering future honey for the hive;

the sun high in the blue haze of sky
sending light and shadow
in patterns on the grey stone wall;

colours and fragrances
freshly manifest among the green –
purple lavender and sage,
vibrant lobelia blue, rose pink.

The young ash waves his leaves
greeting the crazily skimming swifts,
muted music seeps from the house next door
and the black cat rolls in rapture on the path.

Meanwhile I sit here
busily gathering words
and storing summer's sweetness
to spread on winter days.

After Ethel's Funeral

I remember it was a bleak New Year
our tyre tracks darkening the road behind us,
stark on the glittering frost,
and the rooks screeching, black among
the spine-bare trees,
making a virtue of death.

We drove to the crematorium
which had already swallowed
two of our dead behind its sly curtain.
That day the furnace was sated
as we circled the frozen pond,
the fountain dismantled,
dead leaves trapped in the ice
like drowned souls.

We greeted the small grove of birch trees
where, if I could, I'd have scattered the ashes,
offering what remained to the care of the old gods.

Later we sat in your sleek new car
sipping hot tea from a flask,
eating our fill of turkey and fruit cake,
your breath quick on the misted window,
your presence an anchor there
in that place of violent dispersals.

I remember the glove compartment closing
with a brisk click, unhinging the silence

and knowing there's not much
between one sound and another

or one breath and another:

just a gap narrow enough
for a life to slip through.

Sybil

Sybil phones to speak to a mutual friend –
now wending her way back
to the Somerset levels –
and stays on the line because, really,
any ear will do, and she talks non-stop
in speech that forks and branches
and flows in rivulets of sound
till I am spell-bound in the labyrinth of her tales:

"I went to see a film at a cinema
by a shop which is owned by a friend
who has a brother I went with
to a concert in 1987

so I missed Sophie's wedding
and was told off by my sister
whom I've never liked
and never shall
and I paid £20 to have her
taken out of my will
which would have been cheap
at double the price

and then I got on a bus
which passed by a park
where I saw a man in a panama hat
I think I may have known…"

She is ended now.

The drugs they gave her left her dumb
and at the close of one long winter's day –
her only language being pain –
she neatly wrapped her Christmas gifts,
laid them carefully on the table
then took the necessary pills.

And was found the next day
lying politely on her bed,
fully-dressed and silent.

Parting

The sea opens wide,
a gaping mouth;
wind-fuelled diesel fumes
molest the nose
and careless water thumps the hull.

Across the gang-plank
voices rise in anguish –
lovers taste the bitterness of salt,
the incompatibility of shores.

Symbiosis

Grey was the colour of the sitting-room wall,
it was stone and once spoke to her
of cliffs and cairns
and the unavailability of history,
carried the romance of wild places
among the stereo and sofas.

But in time it oppressed her;
the greyness trickled its way
into small crevices inside her
and bled the plushy softness
of her plum-ripe days.

Like stone axes her thoughts
sharpened and narrowed until,
once generous, she gave now
with flinty hands
and lanced emerging friendships
with a stare.

For the Ancestors

at Nos Galan Gaeaf

As the hours tick beyond autumn
and winter shadows the far hill,
bats gather where once swallows played
and the birch lets fall her golden leaves.

I sit with you, silent ones, to share this meal,
however harsh our words once were,
however discrete our worlds,
they leach now, one into the other –
a gentle confluence –
and like blood the dark ale
carries your spirits
to rest in this small circle of light;
united we gather strength to nurture
whatever future may be born
and bless the ones who are to come.

Outside, the marigolds glare down
the coming dark
while beyond the river,
the crane is flying with my wings.

If I Were A Snake

If I were a snake I could shed my skin easily,
no, not easily perhaps, but quickly,
it would be like taking off a tight coat
in a small space
and being revealed in my smartest clothes,
freshly-purchased, cool and colourful,
ready to introduce myself again,
a re-invention.

If I were a snake, I'd think little of it,
I'd have been born with an instinct for change,
a talent for it, I'd have moved swiftly
through all manner of deaths and entrances.

But being human my skin sheds differently;
it scales, exfoliates,
delicately, in its own time,
as soft and silent in its falling
as flakes of snow.
Long before death, parts of my body
have become dust,
hovering and settling around me,
particles of the past.

Being human, shedding my whole skin
would be violent – unviable.
Imagine uncovering the dark and secret
throbbing of the heart,
the lungs' bloody, tidal rhythm.
How could I survive without a barrier of skin,
of soft and subtle hide?

I choose then the human way,
to move towards this new beginning,
with gossamer steps,
an unfurling so gradual
that time itself seems frozen.

As gently and silently as drifting snow,
I move out of my old skin,
discard the past,
let it hover, then disperse,
lightly dusting the future.

Daisy

a child's garland
the day's eye
opens in wonder

 the door blows open
sunlight rolls a golden carpet
    down the hall

courting sparrow
his drab plumage
takes a shine

     in the stream
     the small stones grow
     to make a crossing place

sentinel blackbird
overseeing the garden
its symphony of food

       suddenly
     a clump of hawkweed
     blazes with summer

          on streams of air
            the red kite sails
          beyond knowing

             a settled mist blurs the garden
                indoors
             the day lacks definition

Chain

scattering rooks pepper the sky
a taste of salt on the west wind –
seasoned days

against the skyline
a row of trees curtsey
their backs to the sea

through the scribbled branches
of the beech tree
the evening sky turns pewter

snowflakes perish on the waves
sun shines cold in distant sky
how its light freezes

bare branches
sweep the sky
banishing contrails

the goldfinch rides
the mast of the evening primrose
a sailor scanning for land

snow-heavy hills blend with sky
merrily
windmills spin their blades

in the shelter of a holly tree
a bush of bright pink bells
remembers spring

Portal Stone

You hold the memory of aeons,
reaching far back to the shaping of the earth,
when the world was seen by other eyes –
non-human.

Of the hardness and implacability of time,
yet shaped by an element
that parts at your touch,

you evoke shapes, curled and sleeping,
of ammonite and sea-horse,
or the mystical egg of Orpheus
that held the seeds of an ancient birth,
spawning a myriad of forms.

Incoming

We busy ourselves in the sun,
tilling and sowing,
our gloved hands brave against
stone and nettle and the lingering snake;
all creation is here, caught in the seeds
that woo the earth with such succulent promise.

Birds blazon their call across hedgerows,
hostages to fortune, they forage
oblivious to warfare and bombing
and the futility of blossom.

Suddenly the gloves' fingers invert and repel,
the future is jilted as something pitiless
falls like ash on the tree-dappled lawn

and running, there's no time to look back
and see how softly it smothers
the once certain feast.

Naming Yourself *(for Kate)*

To be named is to be called to exist;
to perch a while in this incarnate world
hovering on the rim of infinity.

To re-name yourself
is to be reborn in your own image;
to emerge newly-fledged

and rise into your own story,
discarding the leaves of a mordant tale
moulded by others.

Take some of their colours –
coppers and gold –
glory in their beauty,
leave behind what is mildewed.

Move vibrantly forward –
like the birch tree in winter
shine silver in darkness.

Await the rebirth of spring,
then take wing into the future
resounding now with your own invocation.

Sunflowers

On rising ground they stand
like Promethean gods,
their haloed faces turned to the east –
ever-attuned to the coming of dawn.

This is their wisdom:
knowing how hope renews
with the return of the light.

Outside León's bar the children share *pipas,*
the seeds of the sunflower,
dancing their spirals among parents and elders,
chasing and chattering in flurries of colour,

"Crack open the husks of life", they say,
"taste the seeds born of these vibrant gods!"

As the waiting hills now flare with gold,
see how joy is kindled,
the seeds of hope resown.

The Drunken Fiddler

"Wholesome," Deirdre would have called them,
these clean and fresh young people
who rise early, wear stout shoes
and, for now at least, follow well-worn paths.

I see him through their eyes –
a drunken fiddler –
oh, he plays well enough
when the drink has loosened his fingers,
but his gargantuan thirst for the dark liquid
is more legendary.

Yet when he plays,
I hear the fiddle sing,
a flowing stream
of sensuous song
that calls the well-springs
of my desiccated heart
to the sea – to the sea.

In the chattering pub we sit together
in different worlds,
for what do they know
of the far and bony shores of life,
where the tide ebbs and ebbs
with no sure return?

Yet I would not be
a creature of dry land,
stepping forth in laced-up shoes
on mapped-out paths
drawn by others' hands,

but rather a creature of the seas,
feeling the flood-tide
of the heart's rhythm,
tasting the blood-red salt
that falls from the stars.

Blessing of the Three Namesakes

(for my grandson)

Like the first Dylan glimpsed in myth
may you swim slick as the swiftest fish
and in the silver streams of thought
may there be none to overcome you, Dylan,
Son of the Wave.

May you be young and easy under the apple trees,
as green and carefree as the poet
and happy as the heart is long;
and may your wishes all bear fruit, Dylan,
Prince of the Plenteous Orchards.

May the minstrel's blessing keep you young
and life for you be as a song
sung throughout the winds of change;
may you always know the false from true
and see the long-time sun surrounding you, Dylan,
Child of my Child.

A Tiding of Magpies *(for my grand-daughter)*

One for sorrow, two for joy
three for a girl, four for a boy.

You were breathed into me
with the chatter of magpies
nearing Coedgenau,
that deep wooded curve
where the road is no longer the highway
but flirts with primitive woods,
with woods of the mind.

I've seen owls there, journeying at night,
once one flew towards me
veiled in white spectral light,
but this was the daytime,
the slow drift of the ordinary,
when a magpie, crossing my path,
was chased by another and watched by a third.
I slowed to search for a fourth, expecting a pair,
but there was no other, just the three – for a girl.

These pied thieves had stolen news from the future
and for many long weeks I carry the knowledge,
catch glimpses of you in the colloquy of owls
and the gossip of trees
or in the late morning when the white flashing
wings of the magpies echo the news,
and black and white feathers fall at my feet.

Leila Skye, beauty of night,
you were breathed into me by a triad of magpies –
but of what you'll become, they gave me no sign.

Rapunzel

*The future enters into us in order to fulfil itself in us, long
before it happens. Rilke*

My room was at the back of the house,
it had a coal-fire and my aunt's wooden bed

where the cat felt safe to give birth to kittens –
all drowned
and she herself put to sleep to make way for the dog.

My window billowed out over the yard –

*"Rapunzel, Rapunzel, let down your hair,
you can escape!"*

We walked on carpets of egg-shells, my sister and I,
at night we lay listening
for the sound of raised voices,
and learnt how to smile when someone was looking.

But the back door was a portal
to the garden beyond,
to the two apple-trees
reaching far and away,
calling me up into their branches.

*"Rapunzel, Rapunzel, let down your hair,
you can escape!"*

I dug in the flower-beds
finding clay to make pots,
peered through the staves of the fence
to the other world beyond –

sometimes made contact with strangers –
a girl with a cherry-stained pinny,
an old woman waddling towards me
in mud-coloured stockings.

"Rapunzel, Rapunzel, let down your hair,
you can escape!"

I remember helping my father to dig,
banking up the dark soil,
and later the bright golden gleam of potatoes
finally freed from the clutches of earth.

I remember too picking the mint
for the sauce, my hands growing green
and electric, strong for the climb.

Looking back through the lens of the years,
child, do you see now it was me,
nurtured on green and on gold,
reckless with the wild scent of apples,
who waited and called at the foot of your window?

"Rapunzel, Rapunzel, let down your hair,
you can escape!"

The Luminescence of Bones

This weekly drive along the Dyfi
reveals again the water
glinting knife-like
beneath the caul of sky,
and once again the winter hills
are smudged with mist.

But see the birch!
The birch are luminous
beyond imagining,
their bare-bone trunks gleam white
against the teeming grey,
skeletal beings, earthly yet ethereal.

Remember this when the year turns
and summer reinstates their transient crown.

Plums

You test the plum in your questioning palm
and with a faint 'suck'
which is also a sigh
it slips into your innocent grasp –
ripeness is all that's required,
defines the moment
when something luscious
falls into your hand
as if simply waiting
for you to ask.

'Dyfi' is pronounced 'Dovey'.

Diwylliant / Culture

Poetry at Strata Florida, May, 2012

I browse the mosaic of the day;
words surf over stone in a proud display
and are tucked under the sorrowful yew
where a poet lies – or does not lie
but duels with a rival in sharpened words.

The past sits tightly under the present
and the arch is a poem that frames the wild,
that delineates the sky,
sheltering a woman, a national poet.

"Who killed the Welsh language?" she asks
but in her, *Cymraeg* and English parley in verse
and she sings of the wind
and the scattering of ashes –
dewch i mewn through the door
into expansion.

Gathering the bones of the day,
I notice my place as a lingering stone
cast in the fourth wall
and pay my respects to the blessèd yew
where a poet lies or does not lie,
while in unmarked graves the princes sleep
and decompose under infinite sky.

Diwylliant, the Welsh word for culture, contains the elements 'un-wild'.
Cymraeg – the Welsh language. The fourth wall – the audience. *Dewch i mewn* – Come in. See: storingmagic.blogspot.co.uk/2012/05/poetry-at-strata-florida-abbey.html

By the Pool at Gelli Fach

Something is happening
and slowly the water-lily bud
rises to the surface – born of water,
how brave its journey into air.

At a pace too slow for the eye to grasp
it begins to swell, slender streaks of white
shine through the restraining sepals
like a bosom escaping a bodice

and as time flows silently on
a citadel of petals circles the centre
which slowly unfurls revealing a brightness,
yellow fringed with saffron –
a chalice, a crown.

Too soon the flower will fold its golden beauty
back to bud and slip beneath the waters
to lie like a tattered ghost –

but for this short time, in raw perfection,
the water-lily reflects the grail.

Shadows

on Coed y Castell

Moving patterns of green
and paler green and yellow,
as sunlight falling quick
through leaves and stems,
shimmers on the wind-stroked grass
here on the hillside.

The sky, blue and still and full,
is wrapped around the contours of the hills,
seen far away, across two counties,
yet bright and clear-defined.

From the leafy wood the cuckoo calls,
but lying here is the lamb,
that we don't forget the presence of death,
a silence not to be discounted
among the scenes of the earth's awakening;
his body, acquiescent now,
lies moulded to the clay,
flesh against soil, blue
reflecting in his eye.

The cuckoo calls from the speckled wood
but shadows fall
through leaves and stems
to lie in secret round the blades of grass,
here, on the hillside.

Take the Sea Road

Go to the seashore and listen
to the voice of the waves
whose journeys are always
longer and deeper than yours.

In their whisperings hear
the sound of your heart
and find in its crevices
the iridescent pearl
whose beauty is never
diminished by suffering.

Take the sea road

float with its rising
and falling;
flow with its tides,
recede and
advance.

Then come at last
to the place
beyond movement,
the halcyon centre
where your journey
finds wings.

The Moon and the Beech Tree

Gently the moon undulates,
caught in the curves of a water-lily.
Sometimes, waiting can be beautiful.

Behind me the beech tree roars and shakes his leaves.
What, I ask, has made him so angry?

The earth moves or perhaps the sky moves,
I only know how much depends
on these silent juxtapositions.

Laughing, the moon slides under a rock,
how delicate she is dissolving into shadow,
how delicious her trembling.

Scintillas of light shatter the water,
the beech tree sighs.

Did I say that sometimes
waiting can be beautiful?